◎ patrickgeorge_illustration

© PatrickGeorge 2021

www.patrickgeorge.com

ISBN 978-1-908473-16-5

1 3 5 7 9 10 8 6 4 2

British Library Cataloguing in Publication Data.
A catalogue record for this book is available from the British Library.

Printed in China on FSC paper.

MIX
Paper from
responsible sources
FSC® C117745
FSC
www.fsc.org

How do you feel?

Patrick George

I feel happy

I feel sad

I feel angry

I feel afraid

I feel hopeful

I feel thoughtful

I feel different

I feel accepted

I feel lucky

I feel proud

I feel invisible

I feel playful

I feel shy

I feel embarrassed

I feel cheeky

I feel bored

I feel jealous

I fee

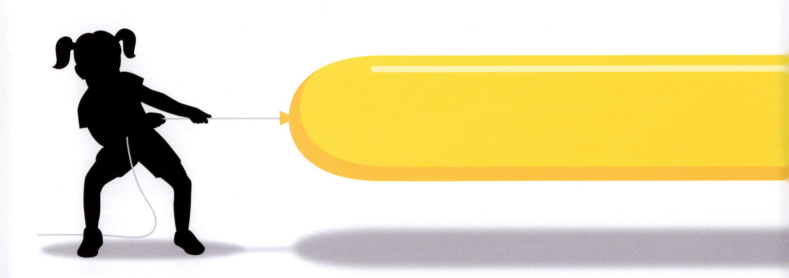

frustrated

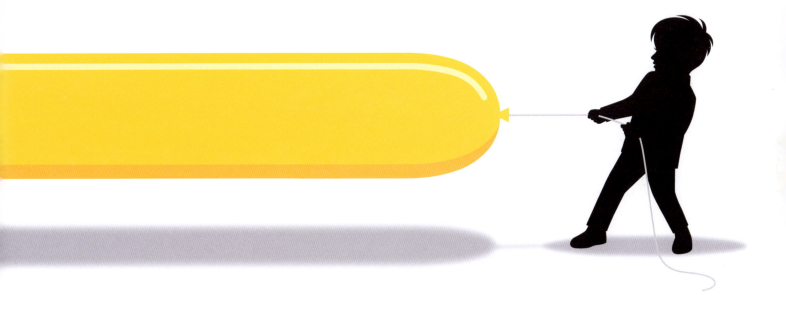

I feel curious

I feel confused

I feel abandoned

I feel anxious

I feel excited

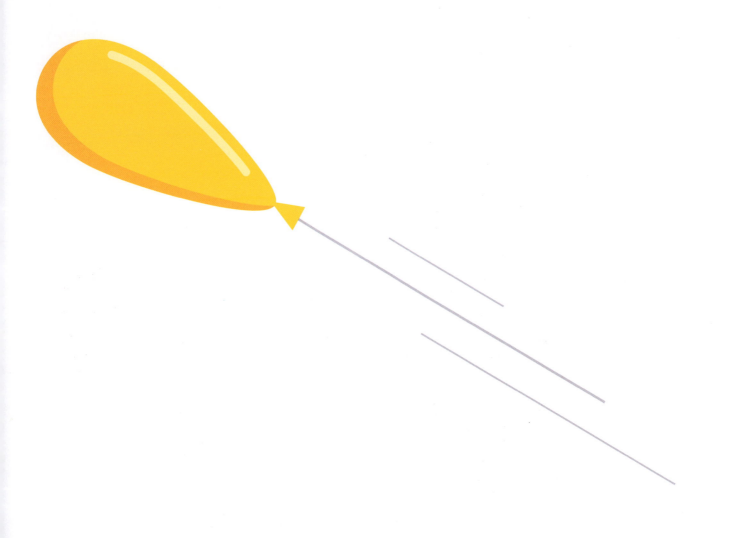

I feel sleepy

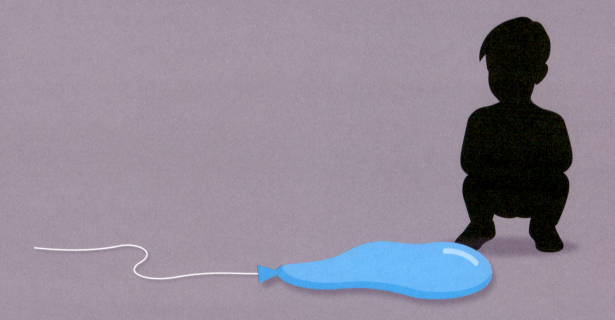

I feel special

I feel loved

How do you feel?